I0409900

Table of Contents

Introduction

Secretary of Defense Leon Panetta stated during the October 2011 North Atlantic Treaty Organization (NATO) Defense Minister's meeting, that the U.S. will no longer be able to make up for the significant shortfalls that have plagued NATO's operations in Libya and Afghanistan and that the Alliance must work together or risk losing the ability to take on such missions in the future. He concluded by stating that with the Pentagon facing $450 billion in budget cuts over the next 10 years, allies cannot assume that the U.S. will be able to continue covering NATO's shortcomings.[1]

Secretary Panetta's remarks allude to the idea that in the future, U.S. military officers will spend more time working unilaterally than in or with multinational organizations. However, this is problematic because recent operations in Libya, Iraq, and Afghanistan are not anomalies; they are instead, representative of the types of operations the U.S. will conduct in the future. Therefore, the U.S. must embrace a future that seeks out partnerships and avoids unilateral action, instead of withdrawing from existing alliances. The U.S. currently fills many of the billets within NATO, to include the most senior military position, the Supreme Allied Commander Europe (SACEUR); however, with budget cuts looming, how well the U.S. will fill its NATO billets in the future is in question.

Acknowledging that not every officer can serve in NATO during their formative years, the Army must include in its officer development model the means for officers to develop the skills required to work with and lead multinational forces successfully. To address this concern, this monograph examines the careers of several officers that have served as SACEUR and asks the research question, what elements of a career prepare an officer for service as SACEUR? The analysis of seven officers, which served as SACEUR, identified similar areas of their careers that prepared them for multinational service, supporting the assertion that an officer professional development model that emphasizes postgraduate education and broadening assignments best prepares officers for service in multinational organizations.

---

[1] Associated Press, "NATO Must Work Together to Sustain Libya, Afghanistan Operations," *Foxnews.com*, October 5, 2011, http://www.foxnews.com/us/2011/10/05/panetta-nato-must-work-together-to-sustain-libya-afghanistan-operations/#ixzz1cy8P8I2r (accessed November 6, 2011).

Literature Review

An unequal amount of literature exists regarding the development of officers for service in the joint arena or as strategic leaders and little exists regarding service in multinational organizations. This reinforces the position that the current officer professional development model does not prepare officers for service in a diverse, multicultural, and multinational environment, but rather for service in U.S. centric organizations. It is not surprising that most literature centers on the joint arena when the population of officers and other military personnel dealing with joint matters continues to increase rapidly. Where joint duty used to be the preserve of senior active duty officers, it increasingly includes officers at the O-4 and O-3 levels. This is especially true in the headquarters of joint task forces and other joint headquarters below the Combatant Command level.[2] The U.S. military has embraced the joint fight and states that every officer must understand joint considerations and that joint competence must become an inherent, embedded part of service professionalism.[3] This methodology is not flawed, but rather incomplete because it does not implicitly say that officers must also excel at working with civilians and multinational partners.

In his essay, "Professional Military Education: Its Historical Development and Future Challenges," Edwin Arnold establishes that the aborted hostage rescue attempt known as Desert I and the invasion of Grenada stimulated an ever-increasing demand for greater *jointness* in U.S. service operations and education. He also highlights that the Goldwater-Nichols Act of 1986 established some specific rules for the education and service of military officers in the joint arena.[4] However, Arnold also points out that although the Army professional education system has developed into a comprehensive system for preparing officers for the profession of arms in the joint arena, it must continue to change to reflect the changing nature of war and society. Noting that the challenge for the system is to identify and implement

---

[2] *Independent Study of Joint Officer Management and Joint Professional Military Education*, (Booz Allen Hamilton, 2003), ES–6.

[3] Ibid., ES–7.

[4] Edwin J. Arnold, "Professional Military Education: Its Historical Development and Future Challenges" (master's thesis, U.S. Army War College, 1993), 27.

necessary changes before the system's shortcomings manifest into battlefield failure.[5] Arnold's insights are useful because they reinforce the position that the current officer professional development model has not changed to incorporate multinational issues.

In a less optimistic tone, James Carafano states in his essay "Rethinking Professional Military Education" that military schools have changed only modestly since the end of the Cold War. He discusses how the preparation needed to fight a known enemy required certain skills and knowledge, and professional education focused on those narrow areas. He also states that officer professional development schools continue to train and promote leaders with skills and attributes to meet the needs of the twentieth century, but not future challenges. His position, like Arnold's, highlights the strengths of the U.S. system concerning developing officers for service in the U.S. centric environment, but more importantly, he also highlights the critical shortcoming that exists regarding the development of officers for service in the complex multinational operations of the future.[6]

In his essay, "Preparing Potential Senior Army Leaders for the Future," David Johnson asks the question, how well is the Army preparing its senior leaders for a future with unbounded dimensions and the complexities of full spectrum operations executed in a joint or coalition context? Although he introduces the idea of officers needing to work within a coalition, he fails to develop the idea further. This is disappointing because he examines the Army's recent experiences in Somalia, Bosnia, and Kosovo to identify areas in which Army leaders were not fully prepared with respect to doctrine, training, and experience. The case studies he utilizes are ideal for discussing multinational operations, but he only focuses on U.S. centric activities. On the surface, it appears as if he considers the need for multinational operations in officer education and assignments, but fails to capitalize on the opportunity and ultimately

---

[5] Ibid., 33.

[6] Jay Carafano, "Rethinking Professional Military Education," *Heritage.org*, July 28, 2005, http://www.heritage.org/research/nationalsecurity/em976.cfm (accessed January 20, 2012).

concludes that the Army should provide greater emphasis to joint operational experience and modify officer education to enhance joint and full spectrum operational competencies.[7]

Cecil Lewis presents another perspective on officer professional development in his paper, "Army Officer Professional Military Education System Reform to Produce Leader Competency for the Future." He presents the idea that the future strategic environment will likely provide more challenges than at any time in American history and that to prepare leaders for this environment the Army must provide a professional development model that prepares them to assume the duties that require senior leader competencies. Lewis states that 15 to 20 years of military experience at the tactical and operational level do not provide the requisite skills for Army officers to perform at the strategic level of war and that the single most important leader competency that contributes to an officer's ability to perform at the strategic level is intellectual sophistication. He further explains that the Army does not provide junior officers with the opportunity to explore and study domains that will facilitate strategic thought or with career experiences that expedite strategic level jobs and internships. In support of his position, he identifies a plethora of opportunities that exist within the U.S. government and higher education system, but fails to consider the need for leaders to gain exposure to multinational organizations.[8] Lewis provides important perspectives that can help contemporary officer development models, and is only shortsighted in his omission of the requirement for officers to possess the ability to work within multinational organizations.

In his monograph, "Strategic Leader Development for a 21st Century," James Hardaway does an excellent job identifying the need for contemporary officers to be able to comfortably interact with diverse populations and embrace complexity. Hardaway is one of the few that has addressed the concept of contemporary officers needing to know how to serve with personnel that originate from outside the U.S. system. He highlights that the current officer professional development model pushes the most

---

[7] David E. Johnson, "Preparing Potential Senior Army Leaders for the Future" (Arlington, VA: Rand, 2002), 3.

[8] Cecil T. Lewis, "Army Officer Professional Military Education System Reform to Produce Leader Competency for the Future" (master's thesis, U.S. Army War College, 2006), 12.

4

complex topics to the final stages of an officer's educational career, and as a result, few officers get a chance to expand their intellectual boundaries through critical and creative thinking prior to their field grade experience. Doing business this way denies the opportunity for junior level officers to develop the requisite skills needed to excel in the strategic arena. As expected, Hardaway concludes that the current officer professional development model must change to reflect the complexities of the contemporary operating environment and that change must occur in the culture and career progression of young leaders preparing for twenty-first century warfare.[9] Hardaway framed the problem of contemporary officer professional education well, but did not discuss the multinational work environment fully.

In his book *Organizational Culture and Leadership*, Edgar Schein argues that NATO assignments are challenging for U.S. officers because they lack a basic understanding of its organizational culture and fail to learn over time how to see the world through its cultural lens.[10] His position being that if officers understand the dynamics of culture, they will be less likely to be puzzled, irritated, and anxious when they encounter the unfamiliar and seemingly irrational behavior of people and organizations.[11] Furthermore, that once officers learn to see the world through cultural lenses, all kinds of things begin to make sense that were initially mysterious, frustrating, or seemingly stupid.[12] Schein's work reinforces what myriad authors have written concerning contemporary officer professional development and clarifies why it is imperative that the Army, as an institution, embraces existing academic research. The work highlighted throughout this literature review is a sampling of the broader collection of work centered on officer professional development and collectively reinforces the reality that the Army must change its way of thinking about officer professional development if it is to meet the challenges of the twenty-first century.

---

[9] James M. Hardaway, "Strategic Leader Development for a 21st Century Army" (master's thesis, U.S. Army Command and General Staff College, School of Advanced Military Studies, 2008), iv.

[10] Edgar Schein, *Organizational Culture and Leadership, 3rd ed.* (San Francisco: Jossey-Bass, 1995), 45.

[11] Ibid., 87.

[12] Ibid., 56.

Research Methodology

This monograph uses qualitative historical analysis to build understanding of how the U.S. Army can prepare officers for service in multinational organizations. The preceding literature review showed how existing literature focuses on the development of officers for service in the joint arena or for service as strategic leaders and not so much regarding service in multinational organizations. The purpose for the literature review was not to expose the existing work as analysis built upon weak foundations, but to show that analysis focused on multinational service is less prolific.

A brief history of officer professional development, beginning with the developments that occurred following the Spanish American War and concluding with the official Army boards that occurred after World War II, highlights how changes to officer development influenced the professional development environment over time and subsequently career progression of generations of officers. This is an important section because it establishes a baseline understanding of officer development in the twentieth century, and provides background perspective concerning the careers of the officers discussed in the case study section of this monograph.

SACEUR is the senior U.S. military officer serving in NATO and represents what multinational service ideally resembles. A careful examination of the careers of seven of the deceased officers that have served as SACEUR, specifically with regard to the variables of education, developmental assignments, executive level assignments, and relationships, provided the data needed to identify what developed these officers for service as SACEUR. Tabulation of this data generated a clear picture of how their careers progressed, what they experienced, and which education model they endured. Analysis of the case study data also uncovered trends that provide the answers to the research question and support the monograph's thesis.

Lastly, a comparison of the careers of these officers made it possible to assess the officer professional development models that have existed over the past sixty years and make recommendations as to which components best prepared officers for service as SACEUR, and therefore for service in a multinational organization. The conclusion provides a brief assessment of the U.S. Army's professional development methodology for the twenty-first century with recommendations for how to improve it so that future generations of officers are best prepared for service in NATO and other multinational organizations.

History of Professional Education for Officers

What officers learn in institutional schools derives from an approved curriculum that aligns with an understanding of the security environment. This section summarizes the essential changes to the officer professional education environment during the twentieth century and highlights how these changes influenced the officer corps. It was logical to focus on officer education before and after World War II because the Command and General Staff and War Colleges closed during the war. The essential difference between the two periods is that before the war, officers did not attend the Command and General Staff College until close to their twentieth year of service, but after the war, this changed to around the ten-year mark. Additionally, before the war, officers attended the War College within a couple of years of their graduation from the Command and General Staff College, but after the war, this changed to around ten years after their graduation from Leavenworth.

Pre World War II Officer Education Environment

The Army has always trained its officers, but initial efforts were sporadic, decentralized, and inconsistent regarding content.[13] Having recognized the importance of combined-arms operations during the Civil War, the Army's leadership began establishing schools that trained and educated officers of different branches together. In 1891, the Army directed each post to establish and maintain lyceums in which all line officers were required to participate by preparing papers on professional topics and

---

[13] *A Review of the Army School System*, prepared by the Office of the Assistant Chief of Staff, G3, Department of the Army (Washington, D.C.: Department of the Army, 25 August 1954), 2.

delivering them at regularly scheduled meetings.[14] As before the Civil War, attendance at these schools was not mandatory for advancement and there was little continuity among the various curricula.[15]

Because of the less than impressive performance of officers at the higher echelons during the Spanish-American War, Secretary of War Elihu Root enacted a series of reforms in 1901 designed to correct the deficiencies in senior officer education that had become apparent during the war. This included the establishment of the War College and the General Service and Staff College. Root also directed the development of a plan of continuing education for officers at all levels of the Army, beginning with the establishment of a school at each garrison that provided instruction in administrative and drill regulations, weapons, tactics, law, field engineering, and care of horses. These garrison schools were a milestone, as they represented the Army's first systematic effort to provide officers with postgraduate education, and they remained part of the Army's officer education system until World War I.[16] Thus, the Root reforms provided the impetus for the emergence of a more systematic method of educating officers in the twentieth century.

The Army had made progress in the training and education of its officers prior to World War I, and those efforts were evident on the battlefield. As a result, the curricula at the Command and General Staff and War Colleges during the interwar period focused on operational concepts such as phased operations, centers of gravity, and lines of operation. Additionally, both schools focused on the structure of large theaters of operations, logistics, intelligence, joint operations, and combined warfare.[17]

The officers that attended the Command and General Staff and War Colleges during the interwar period benefited from the curriculum built upon the lessons captured from World War I and the Army's

---

[14] Edward M. Coffman, *The Old Army: A Portrait of the American Army in Peacetime, 1784–1898* (New York: Oxford University Press, 1986), 276–7.

[15] Kelly C. Jordan, *The Yin and Yang of Junior Officer Learning: The Historical Development of the Army's Institutional Education Program for Captains* (Arlington, VA: The Association of the United States Army, 2004), 4.

[16] *A Review of the Army School System*, prepared by the Office of the Assistant Chief of Staff, G3, Department of the Army (Washington, D.C.: Department of the Army, 25 August 1954), 3.

[17] Michael R. Matheny, *Carrying the War to the Enemy: American Operational Art to 1945* (University of Oklahoma Press: Norman, 2011), xvii.

overall requirement to defend the Philippines and fight a potential war in the Pacific against the Japanese.[18] At the end of the interwar period, officers educated in this era saw the American way of war as expeditionary oriented by using the joint force, dependent on mass, and backed by an expertise in logistics.[19] Ultimately, this system trained and educated all officers until the mobilization immediately prior to World War II and drew heavily from the theories of Carl von Clausewitz and Antoine Jomini.[20]

Post World War II Officer Education Environment

Because of its experiences in World War II, the Army convened a series of boards and conducted a number of studies to examine the training and education of officers. The majority of the Army's significant decisions regarding its officer education system appeared in the findings and recommendations of those boards and studies, and the resulting decisions had lasting impacts on the development of the Army's system of schools and officer education over the next 65 years.[21]

In 1946, Lieutenant General Leonard T. Gerow presided over the War Department Military Education Board, also known as the Gerow Board. The Gerow Board's task was to recommend what the postwar officer educational system should become.[22] The Gerow Board stated that education when coupled with actual duty in command and staff positions should insure the development of officers capable of efficient leadership in the preparation for war, the prosecution of war, and the execution of responsibilities of the Armed Forces after cessation of hostilities.[23] The board recommended three radical recommendations regarding the military's institutional schools.

---

[18] Ibid.

[19] Ibid., 89–90.

[20] Jordan, *The Yin and Yang of Junior Officer Learning: The Historical Development of the Army's Institutional Education Program for Captains*, 4.

[21] Ibid., 5–6.

[22] *Report of the Department of the Army Board on Educational System for Officers,* (Fort Leavenworth, KS: U.S. Army Command and General Staff College, 1949), hereinafter referred to as the Gerow Board Report.

[23] Gerow Board Report, 5.

The first recommendation called for the Army War College to remain closed and for its mission to transfer to a newly created National Security University.[24] The board's purpose for recommending the creation of the National Security University was to eliminate service centric senior leader schools and introduce a joint school system that could capitalize on the lessons learned from the war.[25] The second recommendation called for the closure of the Army and Navy Staff Colleges and the creation of a new Armed Forces College. The recommended mission for the Armed Forces College was to provide officers with instructions on how to insure the efficient establishment and direction of major theaters of war, to include the most effective means through which to employ strategic, operational, and tactical forces assigned to a theater of operations.[26] The last recommendation called for the authorization to increase attendance at civilian educational institutions and to permit full use of these schools in the educational system of the military.[27] The board found that there were only a handful of officers attending civilian institutions and that by increasing attendance at civilian institutions the relationship and linkages to civilian society would remain strong. Ultimately, the board was consistent in its recommendations and attempted to introduce a joint flavoring throughout the officer education system.

In 1949, the U.S. Army followed the War Department Military Education Board with an Army specific review board, led by Lieutenant General Manton S. Eddy. The board's work resolved itself into examining gaps or overlaps in the present system with particular attention to the adequacy of the scopes, missions, and curricula of the various schools to meet current and future educational requirements of the Army officer.[28] The Eddy Board recommended significant changes to the curriculum and structure of the Command and General Staff College. Of note, the board recommended that attendance should be selective and that the course should last approximately ten months and that, its curriculum should include

---

[24] Ibid., 27.

[25] Ibid.

[26] Ibid., 37.

[27] Ibid., 88.

[28] *Report of the Department of the Army Board on Educational System for Officers* (Fort Leavenworth, KS: U.S. Army Command and General Staff College, 1949).

instruction on the duties of the commander and general staff of the division, corps, and army levels.[29] The Eddy Board also made recommendations regarding the subjects taught in officer schools. Specifically, emphasis on adding the fields of business management, atomic energy, and future aspects of warfare displayed the progressive tendencies of the establishment following the war. Lastly, the Eddy Board, like the Gerow Board, placed greater emphasis on the joint aspects of all military operations, with due caution that courses currently given at the new joint schools were not unduly paralleled or overlapped.[30]

The Williams Board, led by Lieutenant General Edward T. Williams, proved to be the most comprehensive look at the Army's school system ever conducted.[31] The purpose of the Williams Board was to determine whether the existing system of education and training for Army officers from the time of commissioning to the completion of senior service college was adequate.[32] While the board determined that the Army's existing school system was generally adequate to meet the needs of the Army from 1958 to 1970, it believed the system could be adjusted and refined.[33] The board felt that the existing system had an improper balance between education and training and concluded that the Army school system should initially emphasize the training of the branch specialist for immediate duty and then progressively broaden each field until emphasis on educating the generalist for extended federal service occurred.[34]

The most significant aspect of the Williams Board was its overarching methodology for officer education. Its stated position was that "once an officer has a firm knowledge of the fundamentals, projection into situations designed to develop his reasoning powers, tactical and strategic judgment, and intellectual capability is absolutely necessary."[35] Ultimately, the board advocated developing officers that

---

[29] Ibid., 8.

[30] Ibid.

[31] Jordan, *The Yin and Yang of Junior Officer Learning: The Historical Development of the Army's Institutional Education Program for Captains*, 8.

[32] *Report of the Department of the Army Officer Education and Training Review Board* (Washington, D.C.: Department of the Army, 1 July 1958), hereinafter referred to as the Williams Board Report.

[33] Jordan, *The Yin and Yang of Junior Officer Learning: The Historical Development of the Army's Institutional Education Program for Captains*, 8.

[34] Williams Board Report, 104-5.

[35] Ibid., 46.

11

could apply their knowledge to the complex situations likely in the future and demonstrate intelligence, versatility, imagination, and initiative in their solutions. The departure from the traditional approaches to officer education caused some contention, but quickly dissipated based upon the reality of the Cold War.[36]

The Williams Board also recommended significant changes to the Army's advanced civilian schooling programs. It reemphasized the need for advanced civil schooling to supplement and complement the professional education already available in the Army service school system. The board's overarching philosophy was to expand the nucleus of qualified officers educated to command, control, and coordinate the Army's progressive exploitation of the physical and social sciences.[37] Additionally, the board recognized an immediate need for officer specialists in geographic, ethnic, and cultural areas of the world where the U.S. foresaw continuing or future interest.[38] Ultimately, the board pushed for an overall change to the Army's culture by urging leaders to usher in an era of officer education focused on developing officers capable of recognizing and coping with the political, economic, administrative, scientific, and social problems of their future duties. Including, strong recommendations for increased language training for the increasing number of officer positions within foreign governments and Allied staffs.[39]

Case Studies

General Dwight D. Eisenhower

Dwight David Eisenhower was born in 1890 in Denison, Texas, but his family returned to their native home in Abilene, Kansas, shortly after his birth. He graduated from Abilene High School in 1909 and worked at a creamery for two years. Not content with his job, a friend urged him to apply to the Naval Academy and though Eisenhower passed the entrance exam, he was beyond the age of eligibility

---

[36] Ibid.

[37] Ibid., 54.

[38] Ibid.

[39] Ibid., 55.

for admission. Impressed with his score on the Naval Academy entrance exam, Kansas Senator Joseph L. Bristow recommended Eisenhower for an appointment to West Point. Eisenhower graduated in the upper half of the class of 1915 and was branched Infantry.[40]

After graduation, Eisenhower received orders sending him to the 19th Infantry Regiment in San Antonio, Texas, and then to the 57th Infantry Regiment, where he assumed duties as the regimental supply officer.[41] In 1917, he became a Captain and received orders sending him to Georgia, to instruct officer candidates. Not long after his arrival in Georgia, he received orders transferring him to Fort Leavenworth, Kansas, to instruct provisional officers.[42]

After multiple assignments training men for service in Europe, he received further orders sending him to Fort Meade, Maryland, to help organize and train the 301st Tank Battalion. Eisenhower became one of the top leaders of the new tank corps, rose to temporary rank of Lieutenant Colonel, and in early 1918, persuaded his commander to let him take the next contingent of troops trained overseas. However, the war ended shortly thereafter, and Eisenhower never saw combat in Europe.[43] He was just too good at training men![44] This statement represents the collective feelings of Eisenhower's superiors during World War I and explains why he never deployed to the war.

After the war, Eisenhower attained the permanent rank of major and assumed command of a tank unit at Camp Meade, Maryland. While there, he met George S. Patton, Jr. and his interest in tank warfare grew from the many conversations the two shared. Both were convinced the tank would play a prominent role in future warfare and explored their theories rigorously.[45]

---

[40] R. Alton Lee, *Dwight D. Eisenhower: Soldier and Statesman* (Chicago, IL: Nelson-Hall Publishers Inc., 1981), 7–26.

[41] Ibid., 43.

[42] Ibid., 44.

[43] R. Alton Lee, *Dwight D. Eisenhower: Soldier and Statesman*, 44–5.

[44] Alden Hatch, *General Ike* (Chicago, IL: Consolidated Books, 1944), 61.

[45] Ibid., 47–8.

Impressed with Eisenhower's tank theories, General Fox Conner brought him to the Panama Canal Zone. Under Conner's tutelage, he studied military history and theory, including the work of Carl von Clausewitz, and later cited Conner's enormous influence on his thinking. In 1925, he attended the Command and General Staff College where he graduated first in a class.[46]

During the late 1920s and early 1930s Eisenhower's career in the peacetime army stagnated; however, he remained in the service and received orders assigning him to the American Battle Monuments Commission, directed by General John J. Pershing. The relationship he developed with Pershing would aid him for the remainder of his career. He attended the Army War College in 1928 and then served as executive officer to General George V. Mosely, Assistant Secretary of War, from 1929–1933. He then served as chief military aide to General MacArthur, the Chief of Staff of the Army. In 1935, he accompanied MacArthur to the Philippines, where he served as assistant military adviser to the Philippine government. Eisenhower had strong philosophical disagreements with MacArthur, but difficult as his time with MacArthur was, this assignment provided him valuable preparation for how to handle challenging personalities.[47]

He returned to the U.S. in 1939 and held a series of staff positions in Washington, California, and Texas. In 1941, he assumed duties as chief of staff to General Walter Krueger, the commander of the Third Army. Later that year after the success of the Louisiana Maneuvers, Eisenhower earned his first star and although his administrative abilities were well known, he had never commanded above the battalion level, and was therefore not in serious contention for consideration as a potential field commander. However, one week after the Japanese bombed Pearl Harbor he received orders to report to Washington. He was now on the road that would lead to Berlin four years later.[48]

On the Army Staff, he was in charge of planning the defense of the Pacific because of his experiences in the Philippines. Marshall recognizing Eisenhower's potential, appointed him as Assistant

---

[46] Ibid., 52.

[47] Ibid., 55–64.

[48] Ibid., 66.

Chief of Staff and placed him in charge of the new Operations Division. At the end of May 1942, Marshall sent Eisenhower to London to assess the effectiveness of the European theater commander, Major General James E. Chaney. Eisenhower returned to Washington with a pessimistic assessment, stating that he had an uneasy feeling about Chaney and his staff. On June 23, Eisenhower returned to London as the Commanding General, European Theater of Operations, and replaced Chaney. Marshall jumped Eisenhower ahead of 365 other officers that were more senior because of his trust in him based upon their personal relationship.[49]

In November 1942, he assumed the additional responsibility as Supreme Commander Allied Forces of the North African Theater of Operations, and in February 1943, his authority grew again when he assumed command responsibility of all Allied forces across the Mediterranean basin to include the British Eighth Army, commanded by General Montgomery.[50] Eisenhower gained his fourth star and after the capitulation of Axis forces in North Africa, he oversaw the invasion of Sicily and the invasion of the Italian mainland.[51] In December 1943, President Roosevelt decided that Eisenhower would be Supreme Allied Commander in Europe for the pending invasion of Western Europe.[52]

Eisenhower dealt skillfully with difficult subordinates such as Patton, and allies such as Winston Churchill, Montgomery, and Charles de Gaulle. He had fundamental disagreements with Churchill and Montgomery over questions of strategy, but these rarely upset his relationships with them. He negotiated with Soviet Marshal Zhukov, and such was the confidence that President Roosevelt had in him, he sometimes worked directly with Stalin, much to the discomfort of the British High Command.[53]

In November 1945 following the surrender of Nazi Germany, Eisenhower returned to Washington to replace Marshall as Chief of Staff of the Army. As East-West tensions escalated,

---

[49] Ibid., 72–3.

[50] Stephen E. Ambrose, *Soldier General of the Army: President-Elect 1890–1952* (New York, NY: Simon and Schuster, 1983), 184.

[51] Ibid., 248.

[52] Ibid., 273.

[53] R. Alton Lee, *Dwight D. Eisenhower: Soldier and Statesman*, 109.

Eisenhower was strongly convinced that the Soviet Union did not want war and that friendly relations were possible. In formulating policies regarding the atomic bomb as well as toward the Soviets, President Truman listened to the State Department and ignored Eisenhower's advice. Eisenhower retired shortly thereafter and entered civilian life.[54]

In 1948, he became President of Columbia University. During that year, Eisenhower published his memoir, *Crusade in Europe*, which critics praised as one of the finest U.S. military memoirs ever written. Biographer Blanche Weisen Cook suggests that this period served as the political education of General Eisenhower, as he had to prioritize wide-ranging educational, administrative, and financial demands for the university. Through his involvement in the Council on Foreign Relations, he also gained exposure to economic analysis, which would become the bedrock of his understanding in economic policy.[55]

In December 1950, at the request of European allies, President Truman recalled Eisenhower to active duty to become the Supreme Allied Commander, Europe, where he directed the buildup of military forces for the newly established NATO. Eisenhower believed that his NATO command was unique because it was the first time that a multinational army existed to preserve the peace and not to wage war.[56] Eisenhower retired from active military service again on May 31, 1952, and resumed duties as President of Columbia University.[57]

The central fact about Dwight Eisenhower is that he accepted the responsibility for making pivotal decisions at critical points in history. The most dramatic of those decisions, and the ones for which he had consciously prepared himself throughout a long military career, produced the Allied victory in Europe. Less spectacularly, but just as resolutely, Eisenhower dedicated himself to the cause of peace and sought the national good as he conceived it during eight years in the White House. He won the trust and

---

[54] Ibid., 117–27.

[55] Blanche Wiesen Cook, *The Declassified Eisenhower: A Divided Legacy of Peace and Political Warfare* (New York, NY: Penguin Books, 1984), 61–2.

[56] *Dwight David Eisenhower: The Centennial* (Washington D.C.: Center for Military History, 1986), 20.

[57] Ibid.

confidence of the common man, both in the U.S. and abroad, and personified the goodwill and altruism of American policy in his era.[58]

General Matthew B. Ridgway

Matthew Bunker Ridgway was born March 3, 1895, in Fort Monroe, Virginia, to a military family. He later remarked that his earliest memories were of guns and marching men, of rising to the sound of reveille, and lying down to sleep at night while the sweet, sad notes of taps brought the day officially to an end.[59] He graduated in 1912 from Boston English High School and applied to West Point. Ridgway failed the entrance exam the first time due to his inexperience with mathematics, but after intensive study, he succeeded the second time. He graduated in 1917 and commissioned as a Second Lieutenant in the Infantry.[60]

After graduation, Ridgway began the long, slow climb through the ranks. His first assignment was on the Mexican Border with the Third Infantry Regiment. In September 1918, he received orders sending him back to West Point as a Spanish language instructor. Ridgway threw himself into the study of language until he was completely fluent. His language skills helped his career significantly, as he would become the Army's leading expert on Latin American affairs in the years to come.[61]

In 1924, Ridgway attended the company grade officer's course at the Infantry School. After graduation, he received orders sending him to the Fifteenth Infantry Regiment in Tientsin, China. This was the finest foreign assignment for a young infantry officer and Ridgway would have the phenomenal luck to serve under George Marshall. From China, Ridgway commanded an infantry company at Fort Sam Houston, Texas, under General Frank McCoy. Impressed with Ridgway, McCoy invited him to accompany him on a military-diplomatic mission to Nicaragua to help supervise the country's election

---

[58] Ibid., 22.

[59] George C. Mitchell, *Matthew B. Ridgway: Soldier, Statesman, Scholar, Citizen* (Mechanicsburg, PA: Stackpole Books, 2002), 3.

[60] Ibid., 6–9.

[61] Jonathan M. Soffer, *General Matthew B. Ridgway: From Progressivism to Reaganism, 1895–1993* (Westport, CT: Praeger, 1998), 14.

process. Ridgway became secretary of the Nicaraguan Election Commission and gained considerable expertise in the delicate diplomatic task of working with another nation, within their borders, and carrying out free elections.[62]

In 1930, Ridgway attended the advanced course at the Infantry School under the direction of his old boss Marshall. Ridgway graduated first in his class and Marshall asked him to stay on as an instructor. Ridgway escaped instructor duty and assumed duties in Panama, after an uneventful fifteen months, he left for the Philippines as a military advisor to the Governor-General, Theodore Roosevelt Jr. Through the influence of Roosevelt and McCoy, he obtained a coveted two-year appointment to the Command and General Staff College. Ridgway graduated in 1935 and after a brief assignment in McCoy's Second Army, attended the War College.[63]

In September 1939, shortly after the outbreak of World War II, Marshall, who was now the Chief of Staff of the Army, assigned Ridgway to the War Plans Division of the Army staff. Ridgway served there until January 1942, at which time he became a brigadier general and received orders from Marshall that he would be the Assistant Division Commander to Omar Bradley, who would be reactivating the 82nd Infantry Division.[64] Later in 1942, Ridgway became a major general and assumed command of the 82nd Airborne Division from Bradley.

The 82nd, having already established a combat record in World War I, had earlier been chosen to become one of the army's five new airborne divisions.[65] Ridgway planned the airborne invasion of Sicily and commanded the 82nd in combat there. In 1944, he helped plan the airborne operations of Operation Overlord, jumped with his troops, and fought for 33 days in advancing to Saint-Sauveur-le-Vicomte. In September 1944, Ridgway assumed command of the XVIII Airborne Corps and conducted Operation Market Garden. The XVIII Airborne Corps also helped stop German troops during the Battle of the

---

[62] Ibid., 15–17.

[63] Ibid., 21.

[64] Ibid., 36.

[65] Ibid., 39–41.

Bulge. In June 1945, he became a lieutenant general and was on a plane headed for a new assignment in the Pacific theater, under General MacArthur, with whom he had served whilst, a captain at West Point.[66]

Ridgway commanded Luzon for some time in 1945 before returning to Europe to assume the position of Deputy Supreme Allied Commander, Mediterranean Forces. From 1946 to 1948, he served as the U.S. Army representative on the military staff committee of the United Nations. In 1948, he took charge of the Caribbean Command, which controlled U.S. forces in the Caribbean, and in 1949 assumed the position of Deputy Chief of Staff for Administration under then Army Chief of Staff General Lawton Collins.[67]

Ridgway's most important command assignment occurred in 1950, upon the death of Lieutenant General Walton Walker. After landing in Tokyo on Christmas Day 1950 to discuss the operational situation in Korea with MacArthur, his old boss, the latter assured his new commander that the actions of the Eighth Army were his to conduct as he saw fit.[68] This was a privilege that his predecessor, Walker, did not have. When MacArthur was relieved of command by President Truman, Ridgway became a full general and assumed command of all forces in Korea. Ridgway also assumed the role of military governor of Japan. During his tenure, Ridgway oversaw the restoration of Japan's independence and sovereignty on April 28, 1952.[69]

In May 1952, Ridgway replaced General Eisenhower as the Supreme Allied Commander, Europe for the fledgling NATO. While in that position Ridgway made progress in developing a coordinated command structure, oversaw an expansion of forces and facilities, and improved training and standardization.[70]

On August 17, 1953, Ridgway replaced General Lawton Collins as the Chief of Staff of the Army. A source of tension between Ridgway and Eisenhower was Ridgway's belief that air power and

---

[66] Ibid., 45–80.

[67] Ibid., 84–91.

[68] Ibid., 109–17.

[69] Ibid., 129–56.

[70] Ibid., 157–68.

nuclear bombs did not reduce the need for powerful, mobile ground forces to seize land and control populations. Ridgway was concerned that Eisenhower's proposal to reduce the size of the Army would leave it unable to counter the growing Soviet military threat. Disagreements with the administration mainly regarding the administration's downgrading of the army in favor of the navy prevented him from gaining a second term appointment and Ridgway retired from the Army on June 30, 1955.[71]

During his career, Ridgway earned the respect of subordinates, peers, and superiors. General Bradley described Ridgway's work turning the tide of the Korean War as the greatest feat of personal leadership in the history of the Army.[72] Ridgway died at his suburban Pittsburgh home in July 1993. At his graveside, then Chairman of the Joint Chiefs of Staff General Colin Powell said, "No soldier ever performed his duty better than this man. No soldier ever upheld his honor better than this man. No soldier ever loved his country more than this man. Every American soldier owes a debt to this great man."[73]

General Alfred M. Gruenther

Alfred Maximilian Gruenther was born in 1899 in Platte Center, Nebraska. He entered West Point in June 1917 and graduated in June 1919 as an artillery officer.[74] In 1920, he arrived to Fort Knox, where he taught military history, courtesy, hygiene, bookkeeping, and mess management. In 1927, he returned to West Point as an instructor in chemistry and electricity, the two areas he excelled at when he was a student years earlier.[75] Ultimately, he served as an instructor at Fort Knox or West Point for his first eighteen years of service, spending sixteen of those years as a Lieutenant.[76]

Finally, in 1937 he attended and graduated from the Command and General Staff College and then two years later from the War College, followed by his first and only field command, a field artillery

---

[71] Ibid., 169–200.

[72] George C. Mitchell, *Matthew B. Ridgway: Soldier, Statesman, Scholar, Citizen*, 20–1.

[73] Ibid., 204–6.

[74] Lilyan M. Alspaugh, *General Alfred. M. Gruenther: Dedicated Spokesman for NATO* (Ann Arbor, MI: University Microfilms, Inc., 1969), 8.

[75] Ibid., 13.

[76] *American National Biography* (New York, NY: Oxford University Press, 1999), 684.

battalion at Fort Sam Houston, Texas. He participated in the Louisiana Maneuvers as deputy chief of staff to Eisenhower. In mid-1942, when Eisenhower went to England to command all American forces there, Gruenther followed as his chief of staff. On his first day of duty, Eisenhower assigned him the task of chief planning officer for the invasion of North Africa. After the North African campaign, Gruenther became chief of staff to General Mark Clark, commander of the Fifth Army, which carried out the invasion of Italy.[77]

When Clark subsequently became the commander of the Fifteenth Army Group, Gruenther remained as his chief of staff for the remainder of the war. This command combined the forces of Americans, British, French, Poles, New Zealanders, Italians, and other nationalities. Gruenther gained a reputation as a staff officer with an unlimited capacity for detail, but at the same time one who never lost his overall perspective. He was a well-known and highly respected military figure in Europe because of his ability to manage the complexities of a coalition.[78]

After a brief tour as deputy commandant of the newly established National War College, he served as director of the Joint Staff and then the Army's deputy chief of plans. When Eisenhower assumed duties as the first SACEUR, he immediately tapped Gruenther as his chief of staff. He served as the chief of staff for both Eisenhower and Ridgway. He had actually been Eisenhower's choice as his successor, but the President and European leaders agreed upon Ridgway because of his wartime command experience and international recognition.[79]

When appointed SACEUR, Gruenther was the youngest four-star general in the Army and known as an officer who could assimilate and organize masses of information and convert it into clear operational plans. His nomination to SACEUR and promotion to full general were truly a distinction, as

---

[77] Ibid.

[78] Ibid.

[79] Official biography for General Alfred M. Gruenther, http://www.aco nato.int/page615131237.aspx (accessed January 19, 2012).

he had never held a major command in his career, having only served as a chief of staff or deputy to other famous commanders.[80]

As SACEUR, Gruenther had to preside over the sharp reappraisal and consequent rearrangement of Eisenhower's initial priorities concerning both the duration of the American buildup of forces in Europe and the nature of arms needed to block a Soviet invasion.[81] Therefore, Gruenther, out of necessity, had to plead with European Allies to increase their spending for conventional forces, extending their conscription periods, upgrading their reserves, and reequipping and resupplying their existing forces.[82] Gruenther championed the policy of the sword and the shield, where U.S. nuclear weapons represented the sword, and conventional forces in Europe represented the shield.[83]

Gruenther's other achievements as SACEUR included a new approach to planning based upon his experiences in World War II, massive improvements to infrastructure planning and programming for NATO facilities, the initiation of a coordinated air defense system in Europe, and the introduction of improved communications systems throughout the Alliance's command and control network. Gruenther retired unexpectedly in 1956. He stated in his resignation letter that he believed that three years was the maximum time for one individual to hold the position if the organization was to continue to thrive under the impulse of new and imaginative ideas.[84] Immediately following his retirement, he became the President of the American Red Cross and occupied his prestigious post in Washington D.C. just a few blocks away from his old friend, Eisenhower.

General Lyman Lemnitzer

Lyman Lemnitzer was born in 1899 in Honesdale, Pennsylvania. He graduated from West Point in 1920. His next twenty years almost mirrored Alfred Gruenther's: commissioned artillery, slow

---

[80] Robert S. Jordan, *Generals in International Politics: NATO's Supreme Allied Commander, Europe* (Lexington, KY: The University Press of Kentucky, 1987), 55.

[81] Ibid., 60.

[82] Ibid., 61.

[83] Ibid.

[84] Gruenther to Valluy, 9 April 1956, Gruenther Papers, Eisenhower Library.

advancement, punctuated by service as an instructor at West Point and the Coast Artillery School.[85] Then

in 1936 and 1940, he attended the Command and General Staff and War Colleges, respectively.

World War II provided an opportunity for him to utilize his talents as an organizer and

administrator. Eisenhower recognized his special abilities in handling staff issues and serving as mediator

in dealing with conflicting interests in an army of allies. Lemnitzer was the preeminent staff officer and

served Eisenhower with distinction in London and in Algiers. Next, he served as deputy chief of staff to

General Mark Clark and to Field Marshall Sir Harold Alexander in Italy. He also served as the

commander of an antiaircraft brigade in 1943 during the Tunisian campaign, but he made his mark as a

planner and organizer, not as a field general.[86]

To advance to the highest ranks Lemnitzer needed the credentials of leadership and so he fought

for a coveted command billet in Korea. He commanded the Eleventh Airborne Division and the Seventh

Infantry Division during the Korean War. He was then commander of the Eighth Army in Japan and

Korea in 1955. His last post in Asia was commander in chief of the Far Eastern Command from 1955 to

1957. He returned to Washington in 1957 and served as the Vice Chief of Staff of the Army, Chief of

Staff of the Army, and finally Chairman of the Joint Chiefs of Staff.[87]

When President Kennedy looked for a successor to General Norstad, Lemnitzer was the logical

choice as he was already part of the administration and agreed with their nuclear policies. Lemnitzer

assumed duties as SACEUR in 1963 and served in that position until 1969. During his time as SACEUR,

he helped implement the new doctrine of flexible response, which intended to reduce NATO's

dependence on nuclear weapons by increasing the deterrent power of conventional forces. His greatest

achievement was his endeavor to keep NATO's military organization intact when Charles de Gaulle

withdrew French forces from the military command structure in 1966. France's withdrawal had the

---

[85] *American National Biography* (New York, NY: Oxford University Press, 1999), 471.

[86] Ibid.

[87] Ibid.

potential to destroy the Alliance, but Lemnitzer's capacity to mediate and balance issues saved NATO. In retirement, he was a tireless advocate for NATO and lectured globally on the NATO Alliance.[88]

General Andrew J. Goodpaster

Andrew Jackson Goodpaster was born on February 12, 1915, in Granite City, Illinois. He entered West Point in 1935 and graduated in 1939 as an Engineer officer. After serving in Panama, he returned to the U.S. in mid-1942 and, in 1943, attended a short wartime course at the Command and General Staff College.[89]

During World War II, he commanded the 48th Engineer Battalion in North Africa and Italy. His combat experience ended in January 1944, when he returned to the U.S. because of severe wounds. After his wounds healed, he worked in the War Planning Office under Marshall, where he served for the remainder of the war.[90]

Seen by many as the quintessential soldier-scholar, he attended Princeton University between 1947 and 1950 in-lieu of the Army War College. He earned an M.S. in Engineering in 1949 and then an M.A. and Ph.D. in International Affairs in 1950. Following his time at Princeton, he served as Staff Secretary and Defense Liaison Officer to President Eisenhower. Later he advised the administrations of Presidents Johnson, Nixon, and Carter. He commanded the San Francisco District of the Corps of Engineers and the Eighth Infantry Division in Germany.

In 1966, he became the Director of the Joint Staff and then in 1967 became Commandant of the National War College. President Lyndon B. Johnson described him as one of the ablest officers he knew and used him to maintain liaison with former President Eisenhower. At Johnson's direction, Goodpaster

---

[88] Ibid.

[89] Andrew J. Goodpaster, *For the Common Defense*, (Lexington, MA: Lexington Books, 1978), 5.

[90] Ibid., 23–35.

regularly briefed Eisenhower on the course of the war and carried back to Johnson the former President's personal advice and recommendations.[91]

In 1969, Goodpaster became Commander-in-Chief of USEUCOM and SACEUR. He was an almost ideal choice for the post of SACEUR. He was in a sense coming home, having served in NATO in its earliest days under Eisenhower and Gruenther. In addition, he had been very close to Eisenhower during his presidency, serving as staff secretary in the White House. That association was not lost on the Europeans, who retained their wartime regard for Eisenhower and their appreciation of his contribution to the establishment and early development of SHAPE.[92]

As SACEUR, Goodpaster received extremely high marks from the governments he served. He made important improvements in obtaining commitments to the Alliance's military capabilities from its constituent members. He also formulated long-range plans for upgrading infrastructure in critical areas and forcefully reminded members of the Alliance of the central importance of solidarity in the face of the numerous temptations to disintegration. He had served during a time of exceptional turbulence, both internationally and in the U.S., and his steadiness and strategist's outlook had served him and the Alliance well.[93]

After retiring in 1974, he served as senior fellow at the Woodrow Wilson International Center for Scholars and taught at The Citadel. He returned to active duty as superintendent of the U.S. Military Academy after a notorious cheating scandal in 1976, but retired again in 1981. Goodpaster was widely perceived as an honest broker, a man to be trusted, and one who was fair and discreet. Former Secretary of State Henry Kissinger described him as a man of vast experience, great honor, and considerable ability. A tireless worker, Goodpaster was utterly devoted to the Army he served for so many years.[94]

---

[91] Ibid., 56–89.

[92] Ibid., 91–104.

[93] Robert S. Jordan, *Generals in International Politics: NATO's Supreme Allied Commander, Europe*, 150.

[94] Andrew J. Goodpaster, *For the Common Defense*, 175.

General Alexander M. Haig, Jr.

Alexander Meigs Haig, Jr. was born on December 2, 1924, in Bala Cynwyd, Pennsylvania.[95] He attended Saint Joseph's Preparatory School in North Philadelphia and then University of Notre Dame for two years, before transferring to West Point, where he graduated in 1947. Haig later earned a Master of Business Administration degree from Columbia Business School in 1955 and a Master of Arts degree in International Relations from Georgetown University in 1961.[96]

As a young officer, Haig served on the staff of MacArthur in Japan. In the early days of the Korean War, Haig was responsible for maintaining MacArthur's situation map and briefing MacArthur each evening on the day's events. Haig later served with the X Corps, as aide to the controversial General Almond. Haig participated in four Korean War campaigns, including the Battle of Inchon, the Battle of Chosin Reservoir, and the evacuation of Hŭngnam as Almond's aide.[97]

Haig served as a staff officer in the Office of the Deputy Chief of Staff for Operations in the Pentagon, and then as the Military Assistant to Secretary of the Army Stephen Ailes. He then served as the Military Assistant to Secretary of Defense Robert McNamara, continuing in that service until the end of 1965. In 1966, Haig took command of a battalion in the 1st Infantry Division in Vietnam.[98] At the end of his tour, Haig returned to the U.S. to become the Regimental Tactical Officer for the Corps of Cadets at West Point.[99]

In 1969, he became the Military Assistant to the Presidential Assistant for National Security Affairs, Henry Kissinger, a position he retained until 1970 when President Richard Nixon promoted Haig to Deputy Assistant to the President for National Security Affairs. In this position, Haig helped South Vietnamese President Thieu negotiate the final cease-fire talks in 1972. Haig continued in this position

---

[95] Alexander M. Haig, Jr. and Charles McCarry, *Inner Circles: How America Changed the World* (New York, NY: Warner Books, 1992), 1–18.

[96] Ibid.

[97] Ibid., 19–70.

[98] Ibid., 155–80.

[99] Ibid., 183–184.

until 1973, when he became the Vice Chief of Staff of the Army, a post he held until the last few months

of President Nixon's tenure, during which he served as White House Chief of Staff.[100]

Haig served as White House Chief of Staff during the height of the Watergate affair from May

1973 until September 1974. Credited with keeping the government running while President Nixon was

preoccupied with Watergate, Haig essentially ran the executive branch in Nixon's last months.[101] Haig

also played an instrumental role in finally persuading Nixon to resign. In his 2001 book *Shadow*, author

Bob Woodward describes Haig's role as the point man between Nixon and Ford during the final days of

Watergate. According to Woodward, Haig played a major behind-the-scenes role in the delicate

negotiations of the transfer of power from President Nixon to President Ford.[102] Haig remained White

House Chief of Staff during the early days of the Ford Administration until Donald Rumsfeld replaced

him in September 1974.[103]

From 1974 to 1979, Haig served as SACEUR and Commander-in-Chief of USEUCOM. Haig

realized the challenges he faced as a new SACEUR and devoted his first six months in command to

inspecting every aspect of NATO. His intent was to show his face and prove that he was committed to the

Alliance. He visited the forces of every NATO member nation and met with the leaders of those

nations.[104] Haig discovered rather quickly that European leaders were concerned because of the Nixon

policy of détente with the Soviet Union. European leaders were also concerned about structure, cost, and

effectiveness of the Alliance because of the great pressure on their defense budgets. Ultimately,

Europeans wanted to know whether the U.S., demoralized by Watergate and gripped by an antimilitary

---

[100] Ibid., 192– 240.

[101] James Hohmann, "Alexander Haig, 85; soldier-statesman managed Nixon resignation," *Washingtonpost.com*, February 21, 2010, http://www.washingtonpost.com/wp-dyn/content/article/2010/02/20/AR2010022001270.html (accessed November 14, 2011).

[102] Bob Woodward, *Shadow: Five Presidents and the Legacy of Watergate* (New York, NY: Simon & Schuster, 1999).

[103] Roger Morris, *Haig: The General's Progress* (New York, NY: Playboy Press, 1982), 320–5.

[104] Ibid., 520–30.

mood in reaction to the Vietnam War, would still defend Europe as if it were its own territory in case of a Soviet attack.[105]

Haig's greatest problem was the overall status of NATO forces. Détente had essentially lulled U.S. and NATO forces in Europe to sleep and this made for a terrible security situation. To remedy the situation Haig embarked upon the ambitious plan of transporting ten divisions across the Atlantic in ten days. This concept became REFORGER, or the return of forces to Germany. Initially scoffed at and deemed impossible, Haig's perseverance and support from politicians and peers proved critics wrong, and REFORGER succeeded in every way imaginable. REFORGER revolutionized the methods of transporting forces and materiel; it also flooded U.S. soldiers into Germany once a year for large-scale exercises in which every national armed force had a role to play as an indispensable part of the whole.[106]

By the time of his departure, Haig had won widespread respect throughout NATO. This was evident by an assassination attempt on June 25, 1979, in Mons, Belgium. A land mine blew up under the bridge on which Haig's car was traveling, narrowly missing his car and wounding three of his bodyguards in a following car.[107]

Haig retired as a four-star general from the Army in 1979. In 1981, he became the second of three career military officers to become Secretary of State, George C. Marshall and Colin Powell were the others.[108] Haig, who repeatedly had difficulty with various members of the Reagan administration, decided to resign his post on June 25, 1982, after only eighteen months in office.

General Bernard W. Rogers

Bernard William Rogers was born in 1921 in Fairview, Kansas. After attending Kansas State College for a year, he received an appointment to West Point, where he was a track star and eventually the First Captain of the Corps of Cadets. Upon graduation in 1943, he commissioned as an infantry officer

---

[105] Ibid.

[106] Ibid.

[107] Ibid.

[108] Ibid., 378–395.

and served as a platoon leader in the 70th Infantry Division until his reassignment to West Point in 1944. General Maxwell Taylor was the superintendent at West Point and asked his staff who was "the brightest and most promising"[109] of the young officers stationed there. Informed that it was Bernard Rogers he immediately appointed him as his aide-de-camp. Rogers served as aide-de-camp at West Point for two years before General Mark Clark met him and brought him back to Europe to serve as his aide-de-camp in Austria. In 1947, Rogers went to England to study politics, economics, and philosophy at Oxford University on a Rhodes scholarship, where he gained an additional B.A. in politics as well as a M.A. in economics. [110]

In 1952, Rogers served in Korea as the commanding officer of an infantry battalion. Then in 1953–1954, he was the executive officer to the commander in chief of the Far East Command, who was his old boss, General Clark. He attended the Command and General Staff College in 1954–1955 and then served on the Department of the Army staff as executive officer to the Chief of Staff of the Army, another old boss, General Taylor. He then attended the War College from 1959–1960. Upon graduation, he moved to West Germany and assumed command of the first battle group of the nineteenth infantry division, followed by duties as chief of staff of the twenty-fourth infantry division.[111]

From 1962 to 1966, he again served in the Pentagon as executive officer to his old boss, General Taylor, who was now the Chairman of the Joint Chiefs of Staff. In 1966–1967, he saw combat duty in Vietnam as the assistant division commander of the first infantry division. In late 1967, he assumed duties as the commandant of cadets at West Point until 1969 when he assumed command of the fifth infantry division.[112]

Following division command, he returned to the Pentagon as chief of legislative affairs in the office of the Secretary of the Army. During his tenure as the chief of legislative affairs, he earned the

---

[109] *American National Biography* (New York, NY: Oxford University Press, 1999), 355.

[110] Ibid.

[111] Ibid., 356.

[112] Ibid.

respect of key members of the House and Senate Armed Services Committees. He then served as deputy chief of staff for personnel for the Army and converted the U.S. Army into an all-volunteer force. In 1974, President Nixon promoted him to full general and appointed him as commanding general of FORSCOM.[113]

In July 1976, President Ford appointed Rogers to succeed the retiring General Frederick Weyand as Chief of Staff of the Army. As the Chief, Rogers focused much of his attention on repairing the army after its years in Vietnam by focusing on training, equipment, and discipline. He initiated many reforms and worked hard to eliminate discrimination throughout the force. In June 1979, he warned that the U.S. would lag behind the Soviet Union in strategic nuclear capability until new missile technology became available and that the U.S. had lost the level of strategic ability to ensure essential equivalence. Roger's forthrightness regarding contentious issues, specifically the ongoing nuclear debate, earned him the trust of the President.[114]

President Carter appointed Rogers to the position of SACEUR in late June 1979 because unlike his predecessor General Haig, an outspoken critic of American politics involving NATO, the President viewed him as apolitical and noncontroversial. As SACEUR, Rogers worked tirelessly to overcome the perceived lag in NATO's defenses; he called for modernization of its tactical nuclear forces, including the deployment of new intermediate range ballistic Pershing missiles.[115]

Rogers devoted much of his efforts to implementing the strategy of flexible response, which had prevailed since the abandonment of the massive retaliation strategy of the 1960s. Rogers argued that the possession of adequate forces was not enough and that maintaining flexibility in their planned employment in order to foster uncertainty in the mind of potential aggressors was essential. Rogers retired in late 1987 after an unprecedented eight years as SACEUR. Rogers, who spent 44 years in uniform, had an unusual combination of talents as a combat commander, intellectual, and diplomat. While addressing a

---

[113] Ibid.

[114] Ibid., 357.

[115] Ibid.

NATO conference in 1979 he said, "One cannot help but to be impressed — perhaps depressed is the better word — by the folly, futility and waste of war as a means of resolving man's problems."[116]

Case Study Results

Before analyzing the preceding case studies, it was necessary to organize and highlight the elements of their careers that prepared them for service as SACEUR. Table 1 highlights the details associated with their education, Table 2 presents their developmental assignments, Table 3 presents their executive level assignments, and Table 4 provides perspective on how personal relationships influenced their careers.

Education, both military and civilian, was the first theme common to all of the case studies. Table 1 shows when the officers attended the Command and General Staff and War Colleges, if they had a civilian postgraduate degree, and which officer professional development environment they benefited from. The striking conclusion from this table is the clear difference between the officers that attended their professional military education before and after World War II.

The officers that attended the Command and General Staff and War Colleges before the war, had no civilian postgraduate education and those that attended after the war had at least one postgraduate degree each. The reason for the change came from the results of the Gerow, Eddy, and Williams Boards. The Gerow Board specifically recommended a focused increase in attendance at civilian educational institutions.[117] The board found that there were only a handful of officers attending civilian institutions and that by increasing attendance at civilian institutions the relationship and linkages to the U.S. civilian society would remain strong. The Williams Board also recommended significant changes to the Army's advanced civilian schooling programs by reemphasizing the need for advanced civil schooling to supplement and complement the professional education already available in the Army's system.

---

[116] Ibid.

[117] *Report of the Department of the Army Board on Educational System for Officers,* (Fort Leavenworth, KS: U.S. Army Command and General Staff College, 1949), 88.

The other significant trend from Table 1 was the amount of time that elapsed between an officer's attendance at the Command and General Staff and War Colleges. Before the war, the average time between courses was three years, but after the war, this increased to six years. The reason for the change again came from the results of the post war boards. Implicit to the guidance presented by the boards was the requirement to balance officer development between educational and practical experiences. To achieve this balance, the Army increased the time between when an officer would attend the two schools. The other more practical reason that officers attended the two schools back to back before the war centers on the fact that during the inter-war period, the officer corps was small and promotions were slow, and ultimately, the Army did not see the need to send many officers to school until another pre war build up began.

TABLE 1: EDUCATION				
SACEUR	**CGSC**	**WAR COLLEGE**	**PhD OR MASTERS DEGREE**	**OFFICER EDUCATION MODEL**
EISENHOWER	1925	1928	None	Pre World War II
RIDGWAY	1934	1937	None	Pre World War II
GRUENTHER	1937	1939	None	Pre World War II
LEMNITZER	1936	1940	None	Pre World War II
GOODPASTER	1943	*1947–1950	M.S. Engineering (Princeton) PhD International Affairs (Princeton)	Pre WW II (CGSC) & Post WW II (War College)
HAIG	1959	1965	MBA (Columbia) M.A. International Relations (Georgetown)	Post World War II
ROGERS	1955	1959	M.A. Economics (Oxford)	Post World War II
* = Goodpaster did not actually attend the full CGSC course, but only a short 3 month war course; also, he did not attend a military institution for War College, rather he attended Princeton University for three years and amassed another B.A., as well as a M.S., M.A., and PhD				

The developmental assignments that each officer experienced, specifically concerning their service as an instructor, as personal staff to a general, or overseas, were the next components needed to help answer the monograph's research question. Table 2 organizes the repetitive data from the case studies and highlights the similarities between the studied officers.

TABLE 2: DEVELOPMENTAL ASSIGNMENTS			
SACEUR	**ASSIGNMENT AS AN INSTRUCTOR/TRAINER/ ACADEMIC**	**ASSIGNMENT ON A GENERAL'S PERSONAL STAFF**	**OVERSEAS SERVICE**
EISENHOWER	Spent his first 9 years in the Army training soldiers, Selected to establish and train soldiers for service in the new Tank Corps (WWI)	Assistant to General Pershing, XO to the Asst. Secretary of War, Advisor to the President of the Philippines	Philippines, WWII
RIDGWAY	Spanish Instructor at West Point for several years	Aide-de-Camp	China, Nicaragua, Philippines, WWII, Korea
GRUENTHER	Instructor at West Point & Fort Knox (18 years total teaching)	None	WWII
LEMNITZER	Instructor at West Point & Coastal Artillery School (20 years total teaching)	None	Philippines (x2), WWII, Korea, Japan
GOODPASTER	Spent 4 years studying at Princeton	Presidential Advisor (x3)	Panama, WWII, Germany, Vietnam
HAIG	None	Aide-de-Camp (x2), MA to Secretary of the Army, MA to the SECDEF, Presidential Advisor (x2)	Japan, Korea, Vietnam
ROGERS	Instructor at West Point, Spent 4 years studying at Oxford	Aide-de-Camp (x2), XO to the Chief of Staff of the Army	Austria, England, Korea, Germany, Vietnam

Concerning service overseas, the trend was that they all served multiple tours in myriad locations. The awareness gained from working with different nations and cultures, many times throughout their careers, provided the skills to understand the dynamics of culture, and be less puzzled, irritated, and anxious when dealing with the unfamiliar and seemingly irrational behavior of the foreign people and organizations they encountered.[118] These skills proved useful throughout their careers, but proved most useful during their tenures as SACEUR.

---

[118] Edgar Schein, *Organizational Culture and Leadership, 3rd ed.*, 87.

Equally important was their service on the personal staffs of senior ranking civilian and military leaders. These assignments placed the studied officers in important positions, but with little or no authority and always burdened with tremendous responsibilities. Additionally, these assignments developed the officers to internalize a culture of consistent smart appearance, courtesy, and tact. For example, General Haig's experiences are not unique, but rather representative of the careers of all of the officers studied. During his career, he was Aide-de-Camp to General MacArthur, Military Assistant to the Secretary of the Army, Military Assistant to the Secretary of Defense, President Nixon's Assistant for National Security, and White House Chief of Staff. All of these assignments prepared him for future assignments at the executive level and contributed to his overall development as a leader of multinational forces.

The most interesting element of Table 2 is the column concerning the assignments as instructors, trainers, and academics. These assignments provided an appreciation for the amplifying power of critical and creative thinking, as well as the need for competing perspectives, problem solving and oral presentation techniques, and the need to communicate through writing. All of the officers gained these skills during their careers; however, the manner in which they obtained the skills differs significantly. Table 1 highlights that the pre World War II educated officers did not possess a civilian postgraduate degree, and that the opposite was the case for the officers educated after the war. When considered together, the data from Table 1 concerning civilian postgraduate degrees and the data from Table 2 concerning assignments as instructors, trainers, and academics, highlights the fact that the officers learned the aforementioned skills from one of two ways. The officers educated before the war learned through their experiences as instructors, trainers, and academics; whereas the officers educated after the war learned the same skills through their formalized civilian postgraduate school experiences.

The Gerow, Eddy, and Williams Boards recognized this difference and formalized it by adding the requirement for civilian postgraduate education to the officer professional development model. The other more pragmatic reason for adding civilian postgraduate education to the officer professional development model centered on the significant changes made to officer career timelines. This difference changed the environment in such a manner that it was no longer possible for the Army to only rely on an officer's experiences during his or her formative years for the development of their cognitive abilities. Therefore, the Army institutionalized graduate school in an effort to excel the cognitive development of its officers. Regardless of the manner in which officers developed, the requirement always existed for officers to develop their cognitive abilities in order to handle the demands of leading multinational forces.

TABLE 3: EXECUTIVE LEVEL ASSIGNMENTS		
SACEUR	PRE SACEUR ASSIGNMENTS	POST SACEUR ASSIGNMENTS
EISENHOWER	Supreme Commander Europe (WWII), Chief of Staff of the Army	President of the United States
RIDGWAY	CG 8th Army, CinC Far East Command	Chief of Staff of the Army
GRUENTHER	Chief of Staff SHAPE (For Eisenhower and Ridgway)	President of the Red Cross
LEMNITZER	CinC Far East Command, Vice Chief of Staff of the Army, Chief of Staff of the Army, Chairman of the Joint Chiefs of Staff	Retired
GOODPASTER	Director of the Joint Staff, Commandant of the National War College	Superintendent of the United States Military Academy, Business
HAIG	Deputy National Security Advisor, White House Chief of Staff	Secretary of State, Presidential Nominee
ROGERS	CG FORSCOM, Chief of Staff of the Army	Director Council on Foreign Affairs

Table 3 presents the manifestation of Tables 1 and 2 by highlighting the executive level jobs held by the various officers before and after their tenures as SACEUR. Critical to the table is the identification that there were really only a few different jobs held by the various officers. This is remarkable because it highlights how education and broadening assignments produced a cohort capable of serving with and leading multinational forces, as well as advising senior political leaders around the world, regardless of their disparate backgrounds. This table also highlights that following their tours as SACEUR, with the exception of one officer that retired, went on to serve in positions of increased responsibility and complexity.

The relationships between Eisenhower and his predecessors played a crucial role in providing NATO with its senior military leader for almost forty years, 1951 to 1987. Eisenhower sponsored and ensured that the right officers, in his perspective, filled the developmental positions required to produce the greatest opportunity for development as a senior leader that understood how to work with multinational partners. Of the eight officers studied, all had personal relationships with Eisenhower, or one of his trusted Lieutenants. Table 4 depicts these relationships, but it also highlights the effects of mentors. The case studies provided perspective on the concept of mentorship because when considered individually there is no context for understanding why it is important, except for that it is. However, when considered across a cohort, and as an integral part of their development, it is obvious that having a mentor, or series of mentors, is not only good for a career, but also required.

TABLE 4: RELATIONSHIPS		
SACEUR	MENTOR(S)	WORKED UNDER EISENHOWER
EISENHOWER	Fox Connor, Pershing, MacArthur, Marshall	NA
RIDGWAY	Marshall, McCoy, MacArthur	YES
GRUENTHER	Eisenhower, Clark	YES
LEMNITZER	Eisenhower	YES
GOODPASTER	Marshall, Eisenhower	YES, but primarily under Marshall
HAIG	MacArthur	NO, but under MacArthur
ROGERS	Clark	YES, but primarily under Clark

Ridgway is a perfect example; he served under Generals Marshall and McCoy as a young captain, who both utilized him for important billets later on in their careers. Marshall even placed Ridgway in command of the 82nd Airborne Division ahead of many other qualified officers because of their personal relationship. Ridgway also had an assignment in the Philippines under MacArthur, which proved useful during the Korean War when Ridgway gained full control of the Eighth Army, something that his predecessor did not have. The Ridgway example is not an anomaly; instead, it is representative of all the careers studied.

Conclusions and Recommendations

Conclusions

U.S. officers must continue to serve in multinational organizations so that they are prepared for an unknown future; however, with personnel cuts looming, how well the U.S. will fill its NATO billets in support of this requirement is questionable. As discussed in the introduction this problem is important because a constrained future will cause nations to seek out partnerships and avoid unilateral action.

This monograph addressed these challenges by examining what elements of a career prepare an officer for service as SACEUR. The purpose of this approach was to develop the evidence required to answer this question and reinforce the thesis that an officer professional development model that emphasizes postgraduate education and broadening assignments best prepares officers for service in multinational organizations.

Examining the history of officer professional development and identifying the different education models and political environments that shaped officer development provided understanding as to why officers have differed over time. This information added to the analysis of the officers studied by identifying the reasons for the educational and developmental assignments they experienced.

The results of the case studies not only provided the data needed to support the monograph's thesis, but also identified other variables not accounted for in the thesis statement. These variables were important because they highlighted the fact that postgraduate education and broadening assignments are attainable in a variety of ways, but also that they are not the only components essential to an officer's career.

The officers that attended the Command and General Staff and War Colleges before World War II did not possess civilian postgraduate education; however, these officers still rose to the highest military rank and position. Additionally, the officers that attended the same schools after World War II and after the effects of the official boards achieved the same accomplishments. There are two logical conclusions that emerge from this data. The first is that civilian postgraduate education is not that relevant concerning an officer's development for service in a multinational organization. Conversely, that the officers that served after the war had better preparation for the challenges of multinational service because they attended a civilian postgraduate program. Both of these logics are flawed however because they do not take into account the details displayed in Table 2. Specific to the development of the officers that attended the Command and General Staff and War Colleges before World War II was the fact that they did not attend school or gain promotion to major until close to their twentieth year of service. The significance of the pre-war era officers is that they gained considerable civilian postgraduate educations during their formative years, just not through the formalized process used today. The case studies highlight that the pre-war era officers all spent their early years instructing, teaching, and training, soldiers and officers at West Point or other military education facilities, and all had mentors that exposed them to subjects that differed from their engineering backgrounds. Ultimately, the time spent in institutional organizations, under the mentorship of enlightened superiors, provided a postgraduate education, maybe not recognized with a certificate, but nonetheless developmental in that it expanded their understanding of a broad array of subjects and forced them to think critically about abstract ideas. The lessons learned from their early career experiences proved to be as useful to their future careers as multinational leaders, as the lessons learned by the officers that came after them that did attend formal postgraduate education programs. This synthesis proves that postgraduate education can manifest itself in a variety of ways and that formal degree producing programs are not the only way an officer can expand their intellectual capacity.

The second conclusion drawn from the case studies is the synthesis of Tables 2, 3, and 4. When considered collectively, the data shows that the officers gained the needed assignment experiences not from a specific professional development model, but largely through the efforts of senior ranking patrons. This conclusion is important because it confirms that repetitive broadening assignments are essential and that senior leaders have always known this, but is also identifies that unless an officer has a mentor that can ensure this type of career, then the chances of upward mobility are limited. This theory must not go unacknowledged because as shown by the case studies, they all gained favorable positions throughout their careers because of their reputation and relationships and not because of their seniority or past performance. The fact that Eisenhower jumped ahead of 285 other officers to become the commander in Europe because of his relationship with Marshall is a perfect example of this phenomenon.

Ultimately, the case studies prove that postgraduate education and broadening assignments are critical to the development of a military officer, and that both the pre and post-war officer education environments produced favorable results. It is therefore reasonable to conclude that dictating a specific officer professional development model, although useful for a number of reasons, does not ensure that the officers going through it will develop to the level of an Eisenhower or Rogers. Instead, the Army must consider historical studies such as this monograph and acknowledge that the development of an officer for service in multinational organizations is conditions based.

The prescription of a regimented officer progression timeline, such as we see today, does not establish an environment that cultivates officers to become the next Eisenhower because the Army does not currently emphasis the importance of postgraduate education and broadening assignments. This is because the Army currently values operational experiences at the tactical level because of the high demand for commanders and staffs capable of continuing the war efforts. That said, with operations in Iraq completed and operations in Afghanistan winding down, the Army must consider officer professional development in the next inter-war period by reviewing historical examples, drawing from recent experiences, and instituting a holistic model that best prepares officers for an uncertain future.

Recommendations

As the Army downsizes and reorients on future security challenges, it must explore new methods for educating, training, and developing officers. Most importantly, the Army must develop competent, intelligent, and visionary leaders for future service with multinational partners.[119]

The Army is attacking this recommendation ruthlessly and in 2010, The United States Army Learning Concept 2015 (ALC 2015) emerged with the purpose of describing a learning model to meet the

---

[119] Maurice L. Todd, "Soldier, Statesman, Scholar: A Study of Strategic Generalship" (monograph, U.S. Army Command and General Staff College, School of Advanced Military Studies, 1994), 40.

Army's need to develop adaptive, thinking soldiers and leaders.[120] The objective of ALC 2015 was the creation of a learning continuum that blurred the lines between the operating and generating forces by more closely integrating self-development, institutional instruction, and operational experience.[121] ALC 2015 states that the learning process should begin upon entering the Army and should not end until departing the service.[122]

To accomplish the goals established by ALC 2015, the Army must broaden its understanding of what a holistic learning model entails by considering more than the Iraq and Afghanistan. It must capture the lessons learned in those campaigns and integrate them accordingly, but it must also look to the past and to the anticipated future. The Army must consider the hard questions like, what other regions of the world does the Army anticipate conducting operating in? In addition, how will the Army operate in those theaters? Moreover, whom will the Army collaborate with during future operations? Answering questions like these will enable the Army to understand the global security environment more completely as well as the requirements it will take to operate within it. Lastly, the Army must analyze the current officer professional development model, with these recommendations under consideration, and incorporate policies that ensure that officers gain the development needed to function as part of multinational organizations.

A subjective prediction of the next war should not drive the way we train officers. Instead, and in support of ALC 2015, the Army must consider revising the current officer professional development system to consider the lessons learned from recent operations and historic periods or relevance, and integrate them into the contemporary officer professional development model. Lastly, to ensure that the Army's future leadership is best prepared to serve with and lead multinational forces, it must make certain that officer professional development focuses on postgraduate education and broadening assignments.

---

[120] Department of the Army, Training and Doctrine Command Pamphlet 525-8-2, *The United States Army Learning Concept for 2015,* (Washington, DC: U.S. Government Printing Office, November, 2010), 1.

[121] Ibid.

[122] Ibid.

BIBLIOGRAPHY

Alspaugh, Lilyan M. *General Alfred. M. Gruenther: Dedicated Spokesman for NATO*. Ann Arbor, MI: University Microfilms, Inc., 1969.

Ambrose, Stephen E. *Eisenhower*. New York, NY: Simon and Schuster, 1983.

American National Biography. New York, NY: Oxford University Press, 1999.

Arnold, Edwin J., Jr. "Professional Military Education: Its Historical Development and Future Challenges." Master's Thesis, U.S. Army War College, Carlisle Barracks, Pennsylvania, 1993.

Associated Press. "NATO Must Work Together to Sustain Libya, Afghanistan Operations," *Foxnews.com*, October 5, 2011, http://www.foxnews.com/us/2011/10/05/panetta-nato-must-work-together-to-sustain-libya-afghanistan-operations/#ixzz1cy8P8I2r (accessed November 6, 2011).

Biddle, Stephen. *Military Power: Explaining Victory and Defeat in Modern Battle*. Princeton, NJ: Princeton University Press, 2004.

Binder, L. James. *Lemnitzer : A Soldier for His Time*. 1st ed. Washington D.C.: Brassey's, 1997.

Brooks, Vincent K. "Knowledge is the Key: Educating, Training and Developing Operational Artists for the 21st Century." Monograph, U.S. Army Command and General Staff College, School of Advanced Military Studies, Fort Leavenworth, KS, 1992.

Carafano, James J. and Alane Kochems. "Rethinking Professional Military Education." Executive Memorandum no. 976. The Heritage Foundation, 2005.

Carrell, Michael W. "Inculcating Jointness: Officer Joint Education and Training from Cradle to Grave." Monograph, U.S. Naval War College, Newport, RI, 2000.

Coffman, Edward M. *The Old Army: A Portrait of the American Army in Peacetime, 1784–1898*. New York, NY: Oxford University Press, 1986.

Cook, Blanche Wiesen. *The Declassified Eisenhower: A Divided Legacy*. Garden City, NY: Doubleday & Company, Inc., 1981.

CSIS Senior NATO Policy Group, Harold Brown, and Alexander Meigs Haig. *The Nato Summit and Beyond : A Consensus Report of the CSIS Senior Nato Policy Group* Panel Report,. Washington D.C.: Center for Strategic and International Studies, 1994.

D'Angelo, Dennis L. "Developing Operational Leadership for the Future." Monograph, U.S. Naval War College, Newport, RI, 1998.

Dempsey, General Martin E. "Our Army's Campaign of Learning." Speech, Association of the United States Army's Chapter Presidents Dinner, Washington, D.C., October 4, 2009. In AUSA, www.ausa.org/publications.

Dwight David Eisenhower: The Centennial. Washington D.C.: Center for Military History, 1986.

Edwards, Paul M. *General Matthew B. Ridgway: An Annotated Bibliography* Bibliographies of Battles and Leaders,. Westport, CT: Greenwood Press, 1993.

Endres, Michael T. "Preparing Officers for Joint Duty: An Analysis of U.S. Joint Professional Military Education." Monograph, U.S. Naval War College, Newport, RI, 2000.

Gehler, Christopher, P. "Agile Leaders, Agile Institutions: Educating Adaptive and Innovative Leaders for Today and Tomorrow." Monograph, U.S. Army War College, Carlisle Barracks, Pennsylvania, 2005.

Green, Gerald H. "Professional Military Education for Today's US Army Captains." Monograph, U.S. Army Command and General Staff College, School of Advanced Military Studies, Fort Leavenworth, KS, 2011.

Goodpaster, Andrew Jackson. *For the Common Defense.* Lexington, MA: Lexington Books, 1977.

Goodpaster, Andrew Jackson, and Samuel P. Huntington, University of Nebraska at Omaha., and American Enterprise Institute for Public Policy Research. *Civil-Military Relations Studies in Defense Policy.* Washington D.C.: American Enterprise Institute for Public Policy Research, 1977.

Grover, Josiah T. "Andrew J. Goodpaster Jr., 1915–1947: The Making of a Political–Military Officer." Master's Thesis, University of North Carolina, Chapel Hill, NC, 2009.

Haig, Alexander M. *Inner Circles: How America Changed the World.* New York, NY: Warner Books, 1992.

Hardaway, James M. "Strategic Leader Development for a 21st Century Army." Monograph, U.S. Army Command and General Staff College, School of Advanced Military Studies, 2008.

Hatch, Alden. *General Ike.* Chicago, IL: Consolidated Books, 1944.

Hohmann, James. "Alexander Haig, 85; soldier-statesman managed Nixon resignation," *Washingtonpost.com,* February 21, 2010, http://www.washingtonpost.com/wp-dyn/content/article/2010/02/20/AR2010022001270.html (accessed November 14, 2011).

Independent Study of Joint Officer Management and Joint Professional Military Education. McLean, VA: Booz, Allen & Hamilton, 2003.

Janowitz, Morris. *The Professional Soldier: A Social and Political Portrait.* New York: The Free Press, 1971.

Johnson, David. E. *Preparing Potential Senior Army Leaders for the Future: An Assessment of Leader Development Efforts in the Post-Cold War Era.* Santa Monica, CA: Rand, 2002.

Jordan, Kelly C. *The Yin and Yang of Junior Officer Learning: The Historical Development of the Army's Institutional Education Program for Captains.* Arlington, VA: The Association of the United States Army, 2004.

Jordan, Robert S. *Generals in International Politics.* Lexington, KY: The University Press of Kentucky, 1987.

Jordan, Robert S. *Norstad: Cold War NATO Supreme Commander*. New York, NY: St. Martin's Press, 2000.

Korda, Michael. *Ike : An American Hero*. 1st ed. New York, NY: Harper, 2007.

Lee, R. Alton. *Dwight D. Eisenhower: Soldier and Statesman*. Chicago: Nelson–Hall, 1981.

Lewis, Cecil T., III. "Army Officer Professional Military Education System Reform to Produce Leader Competency for the Future." Monograph, U.S. Army War College, Carlisle Barracks, Pennsylvania, 2006.

Matheny, Michael R. *Carrying the War to the Enemy: American Operational Art to 1945*. Norman: University of Oklahoma Press, 2011.

McGuire, Mark, A. "Senior Officers and Strategic Leader Development." *Joint Forces Quarterly JFQ,* no. 29 (Autumn/Winter 2001-02): 91–96.

McCausland, Jeffrey, D. and Martin, Gregg, F. "Transforming Strategic Leader Education for the 21st Century Army." *Parameters* (Autumn 2001) 17–33.

Mitchell, George C. *Matthew B. Ridgway : Soldier, Statesman, Scholar, Citizen*. Mechanicsburg, PA: Stackpole Books, 2002.

Morris, Roger. *Haig, the General's Progress*. 1st ed. New York, NY: Playboy Press, 1982.

NATO Handbook. Brussels, BE: NATO Information Service, 2006.

Norris, Frank W., Major General, USA. *Review of Army Officer Education System,* 3 vols. Washington, D.C.: Department of the Army, 1971.

Norris, John G. "Is Professional Military Education preparing BCT Commanders for command in the 21st Century?" Monograph, U.S. Army War College, Carlisle Barracks, Pennsylvania, 2008.

Pierce, James G. "Is the Organizational Culture of the U.S. Army Congruent with the Professional Development of Its Senior Level Officer Corps?" *Letort Papers*. Carlisle, PA: Strategic Studies Institute, U.S. Army War College, 2010.

Radin, Beryl. *The Accountable Juggler: The Art of Leadership in a Federal Agency*. Washington D.C.: CQ Press, 2002.

Reed, George, Craig Bullis, Ruth Collins, and Christopher Paparone. "Mapping the Route of Leadership Education Caution Ahead." *Parameters* Vol. XXXIV (Autumn 2004): 46–60.

Ridgway, Matthew B. *Soldier: The Memoirs of Matthew B. Ridgway*. New York, NY: Harper & Brothers, 1956.

Schein, Edgar. *Organizational Culture and Leadership*, 3rd ed. San Francisco, CA: Jossey-Bass, 2004.

43

Schifferle, Peter J. *America's School For War: Fort Leavenworth, Officer Education, and Victory in World War II.* Lawrence, KS: University Press of Kansas, 2010.

Soffer, Jonathan M. *General Matthew B. Ridgway : From Progressivism to Reaganism, 1895-1993.* Westport, Conn.: Praeger, 1998.

Todd, Maurice L. "Soldier, Statesman, Scholar: A Study of Strategic Generalship." Monograph, U.S. Army Command and General Staff College, School of Advanced Military Studies, 1994.

U.S. Department of the Army. *Army Leaders for the 21st Century Final Report,*: Headquarters, Department of the Army, Deputy Chief of Staff, G-3/5/7, Washington, D.C.: 22 November 2006.

_____. *Army Leadership.* FM 6-22. Washington, D.C.: 2006.

_____. *Army Posture Statement 2007. A Campaign Quality Army with Joint and Expeditionary Capabilities.*: Washington, D.C.: http://www.army.mil/aps/07, Department of the Army, 2007.

_____. *Army Training and Leader Development.* Army Regulation 350-1. Washington, D.C.: 2010.

_____. *Army Training and Leader Development Panel Officer Study Report to the Army (ATLDP).* Washington D.C.: U.S.Army, 2002. http://www.army.mil/atld. (accessed November 15, 2007).

_____. *Commissioned Officer Professional Development and Career Management.* Department of the Army Pamphlet 600-3. Washington, DC: U.S. Government Printing Office, 2010.

_____. *Institutional Leader Training and Education.* TRADOC Regulation 350-10.:Fort Monroe, Virginia, 12 August 2002.

_____. *Leader Development for America's Army.* Department of the Army Pamphlet 350-58. Washington, DC: U.S. Government Printing Office, 1994.

_____. *Officer Personnel Management System XXI Study Final Report,* 4 vols. Washington, D.C.: Department of the Army, July 1997.

_____. *Professional Development of Officers Study,* 5 vols. Lieutenant General Charles W. Bagnal, director. Washington, D.C.: Head Quarters, Department of the Army, Officer of the Chief of Staff, 1985.

_____. *Report of the Department of the Army Board on Educational System for Officers.* Fort Leavenworth, Kansas: US Army Command and General Staff College, 1949.

_____. *Report of the Department of the Army Board on Educational System for Officers.* Memorandum from the Office of The Adjutant General, Department of the Army, 1951.

_____. *Report of the Department of the Army Board to Review Army Officer Schools,* 4 vols. Washington DC: Department of the Army, 1966.

_____. *Report of the Department of the Army Officer Education and Training Review Board.* Washington DC: Department of the Army, 1958.

_____. *Report of War Department Military Education Board on Educational System for Officers of the Army.* Fort Leavenworth, KS: US Army Command and General Staff College, 1946.

_____. *The United States Army Learning Concept for 2015.* Training and Doctrine Command Pamphlet 525-8-2. Washington, DC: U.S. Government Printing Office, 2010.

US House. Committee on Armed Services Subcommittee on Oversight and Investigations. *Another Crossroads? Professional Military Education Two Decades After the Goldwater-Nichols Act and the Skelton Panel.* 111th Cong., 2d session., 2010. Committee Print, 111–4.

U.S. Institute of Higher Defense Studies. Capstone, Syllabus, General and Flag Officer Professional Military Education Courses, Joint and Combined Studies. Washington D.C.: National Defense University, 1985.

Van Creveld, Martin L. The Training of Officers: From Military Professionalism to Irrelevance. New York, NY: Free Press: Collier Macmillan, 1990.

Wendt, Lars A. "The Developmental Gap in Army Officer's Education and Training for the Future Force." Monograph, U.S. Army Command and General Staff College, School of Advanced Military Studies, 2004.

What is NATO?: An Introduction to the Transatlantic Alliance. Brussels, BE: NATO Information Service, 2011.

Wong, Leonard. *Strategic Leadership Competencies.* Carlisle, PA: Strategic Studies Institute, U.S. Army War College, 2003.

Woodward, Bob. *Shadow: Five Presidents and the Legacy of Watergate.* New York, NY: Simon & Schuster, 1999.

www.ingramcontent.com/pod-product-compliance
Lightning Source LLC
Chambersburg PA
CBHW081757280526
45789CB00008B/2892